Oriental Splendour

...an
...or
...nd

Cake sizes
Top tier: 15cm/6in
(Board size 20/8in drum)

Middle tier: 20cm/8in
(Board size 25cm/10in drum)

Base: 25cm/10in
(Board size 35cm/14in drum)

Separator boards between middle and top tiers;
15cm/6in and 20cm/8in round drum
Edges covered with ribbon.

Completing the cakes
Cover the cakes with almond paste and allow it to dry. If using Madeira cake coat with a thin layer of butter cream. Apply sugarpaste. Allow it to dry. Roll out a strip of sugarpaste to cover the base board on each tier. After covering the cake insert five plastic supports on the bottom and middle tiers to support the weight of the cake when stacked.

1 Roll out modelling paste to a thickness of 1.5mm. Lightly dust the cutting edge of the oriental cutter with cornflour. Cut out, then smooth the back of the cutter with your thumb to ensure a clean edge. Cut five further pieces and place these under a piece of plastic sheeting to prevent drying out.

2 Place the cut out oriental design onto a Cel pad. Use the pointed end of a veining tool to mark the details on the paste. Ensure that you keep a forty five degree angle on the veining tool as you make the indentations.

3 It is advisable to apply the colour with the cut out section resting on a piece of kitchen paper. Using a flat chisel brush carefully apply the cantaloupe lustre colour to the top section. Apply avocado green colour, brushing outwards to the bottom section.

4 For each tier roll out a strip of half sugarpaste and half modelling paste mixed together long enough to go around the circumference of each cake. Brush over the paste with avocado lustre powder, then roll over with the filigree side design roller texture. Trim the width of the paste, roll up and then apply around the base of each cake.

5 Secure each of the oriental cut out pieces to the side of the cake with soft royal icing. Use a no.1 tube to pipe the dot design on each side of the cake, and with a damp paint brush remove any peaks.

6 A variation can be achieved by cutting out textured paste with the oriental and tulip cutters and applying lustre powder. Roll teardrop pieces of modelling paste and arrange either side with the tulip shape in the centre.

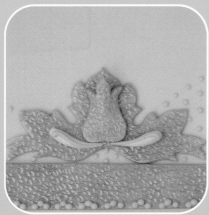

7 Place the tulip cut out in the centre of each oriental shape securing with royal icing the tear drop shapes on opposite sides. Gently lift forward the middle section of the tulip cut out.

8 Cut out one 8.5cm and two 5.5cm hexagonals from pastillage. Cut out three pieces using the entwined cutter and brush with orange pearl lustre. Roll centre piece and texture with veining tool. Assemble the entwined pieces around the centre and secure orchids between, when dry.

Decadance

The round and oval cake shapes allow a contrast of different textures and techniques to be applied which would be suitable for a wedding or special celebration.

Cake sizes
Top tier: round 15cm/6in
(Board size Round 20cm/8in thin board.)

Base: oval 26cm/10in
(Board size Oval 38cm/15in drum)

Completing the cakes
If using Madeira cake, cover with a thin coating of butter cream prior to coating with sugar paste.
For fruitcakes, cover with almond paste then allow to dry.
A strip of coloured paste is used around the base of each cake. Trim the boards with ribbon and stage with your choice of separator. Co-ordinate the top of the cake with sugar, silk or real flowers.

Tip
After rolling out the paste to the correct thickness for the textured ivy, lightly dust the work surface with corn flour. Slide a thin palette knife underneath before you roll over with the ivy texture.

Roll out white sugarpaste for the top tier. Cover the cake ensuring that there are no air bubbles or marks on the surface of the paste. Use a square clear view embosser and apply an even but firm pressure as you imprint the design on to the side of the cake.

Use soft white royal icing with a no.1 tube. Place the cake on a tilting turntable with it tilting away from you. Pressure pipe the first teardrop shape into the bottom part of each square, taking care to taper each. Continue around the side of the cake. Repeat for the second and third tear drops in decreasing sizes.

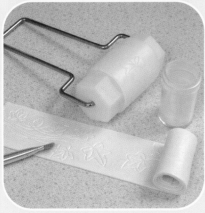

Roll out a strip of modelling paste 1.5mm thick and long enough to go around the circumference of the cake. Apply the ivy texture. Trim along the sides of the textured band with a pizza wheel. Brush with super pearl lustre powder, then roll up like a Swiss roll. Place onto a small cake drum as you unwind and secure to the side of the cake.

Dilute spring green powder colour with water. Position the cake onto a turntable, tilting away from you. Paint the diluted colour onto each ivy leaf. Pipe beadwork at the base of the bottom tier with white royal icing using a no.1 tube and the scroll design above the ivy band.

5 Roll out white flower paste, then cut eight shapes with a small daisy cutter. Use a scalpel to make a cut down the centre of each petal. Cover the cut out shapes with plastic sheet until you work on them.

6 Using the pointed end of a veining tool press down onto each petal to widen and texture. Take a small ball of paste. Flatten slightly. Using the pointed end of the veining tool in an upright position indent many times to make the centre of the gerbera. Secure with sugar glue to the flower centre.

7 Use soft royal icing with a no.1 tube to pipe the small headed stamens around the centre of the flower. Pipe each stamen pulling the tube upwards as you release the pressure on the piping bag. Allow to dry. Apply yellow colour dust to the outer petals and tangerine to the centre using a flat dry brush.

8 *Variation* Use the ivy texture to give a Christmas theme. Paint the ivy leaves with gold powder diluted with alcohol. Stamp out holly leaves, colour dust when dry. Make small berries, and fir cones by cutting around a small cone of paste with scissors. Secure to the side of the cake with soft royal icing. Complement with seasonal flowers or lettering.

Love Entwined

A two tier cake made from a 30cm /12 in round cake. Place a 15cm / 6in cake tin in the centre of the 30cm / 12in cake tin . Line the outside of the 15cm / 6in tin with silicone paper. Fill with either rich fruitcake or Madeira cake mixture. Bake as normal allowing the cakes to cool before turning out of the tin.

Cake sizes
Top tier: round 15cm/6in
(Board size round 20cm/8in drum)

Base: round 30cm/12in
(Board size round 40cm/16in drum)

Completing the cakes

Cover the cakes with almond paste by rolling out the paste at least an extra 10cm larger than required for the bottom tier. Make a cross cut in the centre of the paste prior to covering to allow for the moulding to the centre ring. Use a plastic bottle to smooth the paste inside of the ring. Repeat with the sugarpaste covering. If using Madeira cake, apply a thin coat of butter cream prior to covering with the sugarpaste. Place both cakes on the boards. Cut a disc of sugarpaste to cover the board inside of the cake ring.

Tip
Dust the cutting edge with cornflour. Move the cutter up and down on the cutting board to ensure a good clean shape is achieved. Tap the cutter firmly on the rolling board to allow it to loosen.

1 Roll out a strip of sugarpaste long enough to go around the base of each cake. Use the entwined ribbon texture of the side design roller for the bottom tier rolling along the entire length. Brush over the surface with white satin lustre powder. Secure around the base of the cake. Repeat with the filigree texture for the top tier.

2 Roll out white modelling paste 2mm in thickness. Allow to rest. Cut out eight pieces each for the bottom and top tier using the entwined cutter. Shorten the top tier pieces at the open end. Colour dust with violet lustre powder. Colour dust the inner section pieces with avocado green, and tulip red lustre powder. Place the cut out pieces under a plastic container until required.

3 Measure the circumference of each cake with a piece of string. Fold the string into eight. Use the string divisions to make a small mark on the side of each cake to indicate the position of the cut out entwined pieces. Mould eight rose garland sections from modelling paste for the bottom tier only, then colour dust.

4 Position the entwined sections around the bottom tier using the small mark on the side of the cake as a guide. Position the rose garland between each. Make adjustments as necessary before securing with soft royal icing.
Secure the inner pieces between the entwined sections on the side of the cake. Repeat for the top tier.

5 On the bottom tier use pale pink soft royal icing with a no.1 tube to pipe a dot, measuring 4cm vertically from the cake board between the entwined sections. Pipe a dot, 3cm vertically for the top tier. Pipe the remaining dot design between the entwined sections working from the centre outwards.

6 Pipe the border design with a no. 2 tube with pale pink royal icing. Over pipe with a no.1 tube in a lighter shade of pink entwining the icing around each shape.

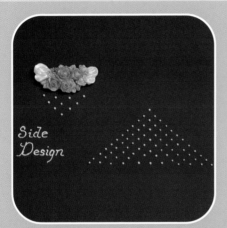

7 Use pale green extra strength modelling paste. Cut the neck of a plastic 1 litre drink bottle into three or use the bottle former. Cut out the paste with the teardrop cutter. Cut out the inner sections, then place inside bottle to dry. Cut out discs 1x 7cm ,2 x 6cm , 2 x 5cm .Cut a 2cm wide strip of paste and dry inside the 5cm cutter. Allow pieces to dry for 24 hours.

8 Clean any rough edges with emery paper. Brush avocado green lustre over the teardrop sections. Secure one 5cm under a 7cm disc with royal icing. Secure a 5cm disc on top, then the ring of paste. Secure the second 6cm and 5cm disc. Make a cone of paste. Pipe with filigree using a no.1 tube. Insert flowers into paste, then secure each teardrop around the top with royal icing.

Summer Romance

A Classic white cake covering provides a back ground for a traditional combination of satin fabric effect, that enhances the elegant teardrop design and a thin satin ribbon which co-ordinates the flower colours for the wedding theme.

Cake sizes
Top tier: round 15cm/6in
(Board size round 20cm/8in drum)

Middle tier: round 20cm/8in
(Board size round 27cm/10in drum)

Base: round 27cm/10in
(Board size round 35cm/14in drum)

Completing the cakes
Cover the cakes with almond paste, then white sugarpaste. An alternative covering can be used, such as royal icing.
Place each cake onto the boards then roll out a strip of sugarpaste to go around the base of each. Trim each board with a complementary ribbon after completing the decorative techniques.

Tip
Paddle the royal icing on a board to remove air bubbles and correct consistency before piping.

11

1 Roll out a strip of modelling paste approximately 1.5mm thick and long enough to go around the side of the bottom tier. Roll over with the teardrop side design roller. Brush over with silk white lustre powder. Use a thin cranked palette knife to slide under the strip of paste then roll up.

2 A 15cm round cake drum is used to help support and provide an even space as you apply the strip of paste to the side of the cake. Bring the ends together trimming the surplus paste with a scalpel. Check that the band of paste is level and secure.

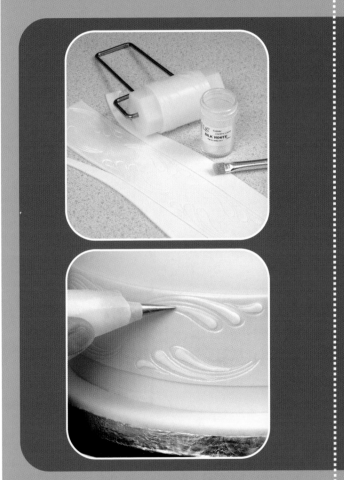

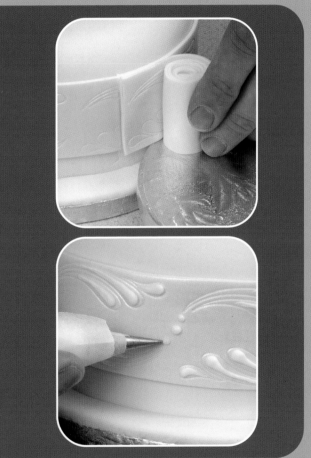

3 Position the cake on a turn table. Use a no.2 piping tube and soft white royal icing to pressure pipe over the teardrop shape. Take extra care to release the pressure towards the tapered end.

4 Use soft royal icing and a no.2 tube to pressure pipe the dots between the teardrop shapes. Make the centre bulb slightly larger. Use a damp paint brush to remove any slight peaks on the dots.

5 Draw a circle the same size as each cake onto a piece of silicone paper. Cut out the circle. Place this onto the surface of the cake, so that you can adjust the teardrop sections to fit.

6 Roll out different cylinder lengths of modelling paste for the cake top. I have not given the sizes, as it is better to shape them to fit the size of the cake. Taper each cylinder by rolling on one end with a cake smoother. Use your thumb and index finger to slightly flatten, whilst still maintaining the teardrop shape.

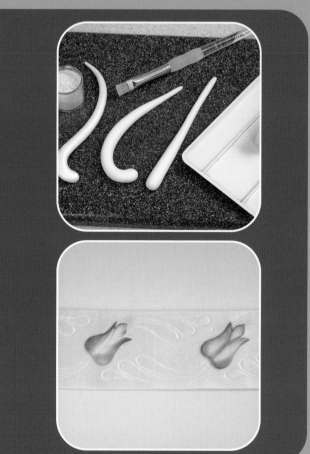

7 Brush each teardrop shape with silk white lustre powder. Allow the paste to firm slightly adjusting the position if necessary to allow for the flower sprays, then secure with royal icing. Repeat on the remaining cakes.

8 An alternative design can be achieved by using the coloured tulip cut outs as shown on page 27. Colour dust the tulip shapes with tulip red lustre then secure with royal icing between the teardrop design.

Empress Gold

Chocolate sugarpaste provides the contrasting background for this stunning three tier display. A gold stencilled base board provides an eye-catching texture for you to feature the cake with something a little different!

Cake sizes
Top tier: round 15cm/6in
(Board size: round 15cm/6in card)

Middle tier: round 20cm/8in
(Board size: round 20cm/8in card)

Base: round 27cm / 10in
(Board size: 27cm/10in card and 35cm/14in drum)

Completing the cakes

This is an ideal cake covering for a rich chocolate cake, which could be layered with chocolate ganache and a fresh raspberry compote. Alternatively rich fruit cake tastes wonderful with the chocolate covering!

If using ganache apply a thin covering before applying the chocolate sugarpaste. For a rich fruit cake cover with almond paste and allow to dry before covering with sugarpaste. Assemble on the cake cards. Insert plastic dowels on the first and second tiers.

✎ Tip
Warm sugarpaste on a low setting in a microwave oven.

14

1 Roll out the chocolate sugarpaste. Lightly grease the smooth side of the filigree lace stencil mat with vegetable shortening and place directly over the sugarpaste. Roll over with a long rolling pin applying a firm and even pressure.

2 Use a good quality brush to brush over the stencil mat with food approved, gold lustre powder. Ensure that you brush the powder between the stencil design, and remove any surplus prior to applying to the cake board.

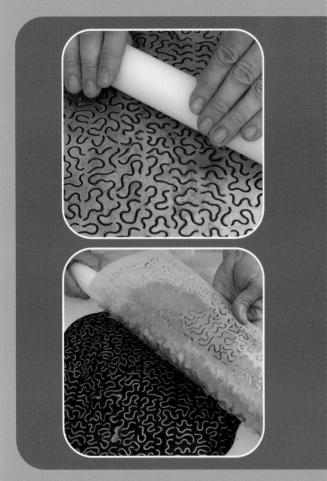

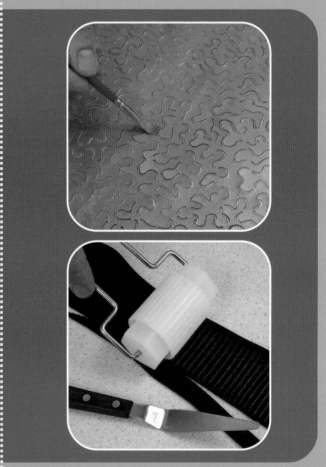

3 Carefully lift the sugarpaste onto the rolling pin with the stencil mat attached. Drape the paste over the cake drum. Peel back the stencil mat. Trim the surplus from the edge of the board.

4 Roll out a band of chocolate sugarpaste long enough to go around the circumference of the bottom tier. Texture with the ribbed, side design roller. Trim the edges of the paste. Roll up then apply to the side of the cake. Repeat for the middle and top tier.

5 Roll out chocolate sugarpaste (with a little added Tylose powder for strength).
Texture with the filigree side design roller. Brush over with gold powder using a flat brush. Using the triple leaf scroll, cut out thirty pieces. Place onto a piece of silicone paper then allow to dry.

6 Roll out extra strength modelling paste to 1.5mm thickness. Cut out with the teardrop cutter, then cut the inner section. Cut out thirty pieces. Place onto a flat absorbent drying surface. Secure the double ended leaf scroll with soft cream coloured royal icing when dry.

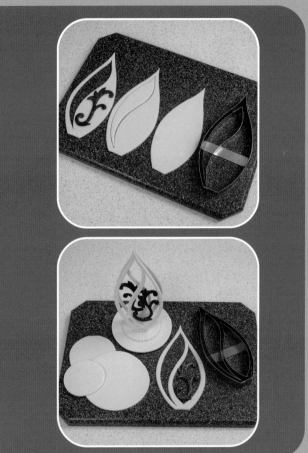

7 Place the bottom tier onto the stencilled cake board. Insert five plastic dowels into the centre of the cake. Secure the middle tier to the bottom tier with a little ganache. Repeat with more plastic dowels. Add the top tier. Secure the teardrop cutout sections evenly around each tier with alternate spacing.

8 Roll out extra strength modelling paste. Cut out the teardrop shapes as shown in stage six, then cut out with the second inner cutter. Cut out one 8cm, 6cm and 5cm round disc. Secure a triple leaf scroll with soft royal icing into each teardrop shape. Secure the discs, then the two teardrops with soft royal icing. Add the finishing touch with a complementary ribbon to the base board.

Lovers Delight

Shades of pink and satin lustre combined with the entwined cut outs provide a simple and effective design for this two tier cake. The use of the crossover texture for the side design roller provides the basis for the additional cut out pieces to be positioned around the side of the cake. If you only want to use one tier, the cake top decoration can be displayed as effectively on this.

Cake sizes
Top tier: round 20cm/8in
(Board size oval 27cm/10in drum)

Base: 27cm/10in
(Board size oval 38cm/15in drum)

Completing the cakes
Cover cakes and allow to dry prior to applying the design. Cut out strips of sugarpaste long enough to cover the boards around the base of both cakes. Apply the ribbon to the edge of the boards after completing the decoration.

Tip
Measure the circumference of the covered cake with a piece of string. Position the string over the "crossover" textured paste to establish the desired joint of the design.

Extra strength modelling paste
Mix 2 x 5ml teaspoons of Tylose with 500g sugarpaste and knead together.

1 Roll out a strip of modelling paste approximately 1.5mm thick. Lightly dust the work surface with a little cornflour, before rolling over with the crossover texture of the side design roller. Brush over with cotton candy lustre powder. Roll up, and apply to the side of cake. Repeat on top tier.

2 Roll out modelling paste. Allow to rest. Turn the paste over. Dust the entwined cutter with cornflour. Cut out using the top two sections. Tap the tip of cutter on the rolling board to allow the paste to release. Repeat for remaining sections.

3 Cut out flowers from modelling paste using the small four petal flower cutter.
I have used 40 small flowers for the side and the cake top decoration. Brush the edges of each flower with cotton candy lustre powder using a flat brush. Pipe a small dot in the centre of each flower.

4 Secure the entwined cut out pieces between the crossover texture, using soft pale pink royal icing fitted with a no.1 tube. Secure the small flowers between the designs and the middle cut-out section of the entwined cutter.

5 Cut out eight flowers from modelling paste using the medium four petal flower cutter. Gently cup each flower using a ball tool. Apply colour as in stage four. Place onto a piece of foam sponge to dry. Pipe in each flower a centre dot with six smaller dots of royal icing radiating.

6 Cut out two ovals of extra strength modelling paste. Brush the edges with cotton candy lustre powder. Roll three small spheres of paste the depth of the small four petal cutter. These will support the top oval.

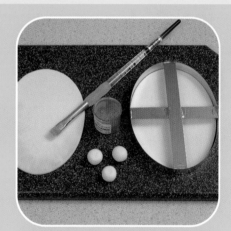

7 Lightly dust the edges of the double scroll leaf cutter with cornflour. Use the cutter on opposite cutting edges to cut out four pieces for the bottom tier, and two for the oval cake top. Brush over each with spring green powder. Apply to the bottom tier with the medium sized flowers.

8 Secure the two ovals with the supporting spheres between using royal icing. Add the small flowers around the sides and the double leaf scroll and medium flowers on the top. Pipe micro dots extending from the scroll leaf sections.

All Wrapped Up

This single tiered cake featuring textured ribbon and the contemporary effect decoration provides an ideal celebration cake for a variety of occasions. This cake could also be made as a tiered version.

Cake size square: 20cm/8in   Board sizes square: 28cm/11in, 30cm/12in drum

Secure the two cake boards together with double sided tape. This will elevate the cake and enhance the stippled texture on the cake board covering. Roll a cylinder of sugarpaste to fill the gap between the two boards, smooth over the edge with a cake smoother, cover both boards with white sugarpaste. Position the cake centrally on covered cake board.

Completing the cakes
If using fruitcake as the base cake, cover with almond paste and then white sugarpaste allowing it to dry between coats. Similarly if using a Madeira cake apply a thin coating of butter cream prior to coating with the sugarpaste.

1 Colour one tablespoon of royal icing with fuchsia pink paste food colour. Repeat for the lilac and thrift colours . Use a small piece of damp natural sponge to stipple the fushia icing over the sugarpaste. Repeat with the two remaining colours.

2 Roll out white modelling paste to approximately 1mm in thickness and long enough to go over the cake from side to side. Roll over the paste with the entwined ribbon texture roller.

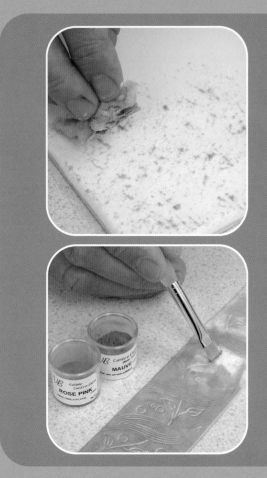

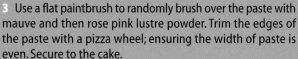

3 Use a flat paintbrush to randomly brush over the paste with mauve and then rose pink lustre powder. Trim the edges of the paste with a pizza wheel; ensuring the width of paste is even. Secure to the cake.

4 Roll out white modelling paste. Using the three colours of royal icing separately, stipple the entire surface of the paste. Cut out thirteen pairs using the two-piece droplet cutter. Cut out seven pieces using the left hand part of the cutter. Cut out twenty-five 1cm circles.

5 Position first, then apply the teardrop pieces while they are still pliable to the top and side of the cake with soft white royal icing and a no.1 piping tube in a random design using the textured ribbon as a guide. Secure the circles.

6 Roll out white modelling paste, texture and colour as explained in stage two and three. Cut four 15cm / 6in sections for the ribbon bows. Use crumpled pieces of cling food wrap to form the ribbon pieces over. Secure the cut ends together with a little sugar glue or egg white. Form the middle section, tucking the join underneath.

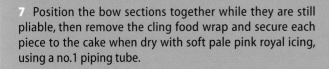

7 Position the bow sections together while they are still pliable, then remove the cling food wrap and secure each piece to the cake when dry with soft pale pink royal icing, using a no.1 piping tube.

8 Variation. The droplet cutter can be used in different combinations. Colour the modelling paste then cut out the right and left hand pieces. Cut out circles then experiment with different combinations of the design, which can also be used horizontally around the side of the cake.

Crowning Glory

A very versatile design, adaptable for any occasion. Add a message, or repeat the design on multiple tiers for a wedding cake.

Cake sizes Base: round 25cm/10in   Board sizes: round 35cm/14in drum

Completing the cakes

Cover the cake with almond paste, then white sugarpaste, allowing to dry between each coating. Roll out a strip of white sugarpaste long enough to go around the base of the cake. Use string to measure around circumference of the cake, by dividing this into five sections shows where the repeat design fits. For a tiered cake, use four repeat designs on the middle tier (20cm), and three on the top tier (15cm). Cakes can be staged by stacking, separators or a variable height display stand.

 Tip

Make the flower dome for the cake top decoration in advance.

1 Work a small amount of vegetable shortening into white modelling paste prior to rolling out, as this will prevent the paste from drying before you apply the texture. Dust the edge of the cutter with cornflour, then cut out, one large , two medium and two small petal shapes. Place under plastic sheeting to prevent from drying.

2 Place the petals onto a cel pad. Using a texture tool, gently texture each petal rolling the tool from the centre outwards to prevent distorting the shape. Colour dust each petal with canteloup lustre using a chisel paint brush. Roll a small sphere for each centre. Texture the centre using the edge of a thin palette knife, then secure to the centre of flower. Repeat for each of the flowers. Allow to dry.

3 Roll out white modelling paste. Cut out five pieces with the triple scroll leaf cutter. Turn the cutter onto the opposite cutting edge and cut out a further five pieces. Place each piece onto a piece of absorbent kitchen paper, then brush over with avocado lustre powder. Remove the cut out sections to a piece of foam sponge to become plastic hard.

4 Arrange the cut out flowers and the triple leaf scroll pieces, as they will appear on the side of the cake.
Measure the circumference, with the string as explained above. Pipe a small dot with white royal icing, to indicate the divisions. This will be the centre point for the design. Secure the leaf scrolls with soft white royal icing, adding the flowers below.

5 Using a no. 1 tube with white royal icing, place the cake onto a tilting turntable, with it tilted away from you to pipe the design between each of the sections. If you are making the cake in different sizes adjust the design to fit, accordingly.

6 Pipe the border design around the base of the cake using a no. 2 tube and white royal icing. Over pipe the design with a no. 1 tube directly afterwards. This could also be complemented if you used a contrasting colour to match the colour scheme.

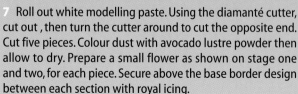

Border Design

7 Roll out white modelling paste. Using the diamanté cutter, cut out , then turn the cutter around to cut the opposite end. Cut five pieces. Colour dust with avocado lustre powder then allow to dry. Prepare a small flower as shown on stage one and two, for each piece. Secure above the base border design between each section with royal icing.

8 Use double strength modelling paste for all pieces. Prepare the flowers as above. Cut out the triple ended leaf scroll. Place each piece inside a half sphere mould, securing the edges of each piece where they touch with royal icing. Cut a strip of paste to go around the top edge. Allow to dry. Cut a 11cm disc to display the dry dome on the cake top.

Tulip Cascade

Colour plays an important part in the design of this square cake and helps to enhance the textures, which have been co-ordinated with the square side design and the cascading tulip shapes.

Cake sizes
Top tier: square 15cm/6in
(Board size square 15cm/6in card)

Middle tier: square 20cm/8in
(Board size square 20cm/8in card)

Base: square 25cm/10in
(Board size square 38cm/15in drum)

Completing the cakes
Cover cakes with sugarpaste and allow to dry. Cover base board edging with sugarpaste. Skewer the bottom tier with plastic doweling. Secure the second and third tiers as you stack the cakes with the thin boards between. Measure with a piece of string, from the top tier down the side of all three cakes. Use this as a guide when cutting the length of textured paste.

Cut out two thin cardboard templates measuring 10cm and 9cm to use for stage two and seven.

Position the cake top decoration between the filigree sections of the top tier. Add the squares of paste to the corners of the base board, to complement the design.

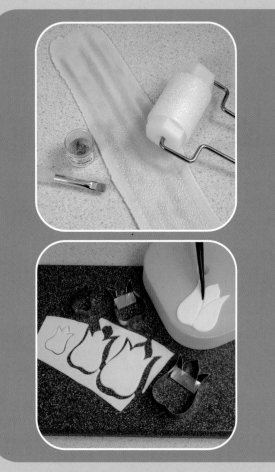

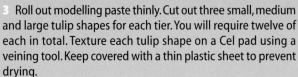

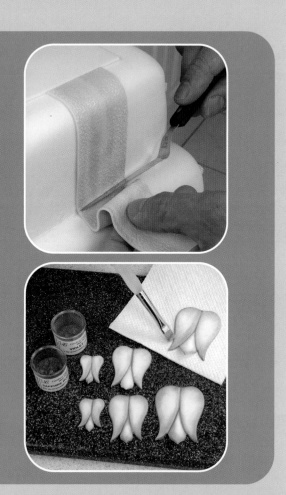

1 Roll a cylinder of streaky blue modelling paste. Flatten and roll out thinly. Use a flat brush to colour areas of the paste with blue sparkle lustre powder. Roll over the paste with the filigree texture roller. Trim the edges with a pizza wheel, ensuring that the edges are an even width.

2 Cut out a 10cm square of modelling paste and place onto the top tier. Remove the filigree, textured paste from the work surface with a thin cranked palette knife. Secure the paste from the top to the bottom tier. Trim the paste so that it touches the 10cm square edge.

3 Roll out modelling paste thinly. Cut out three small, medium and large tulip shapes for each tier. You will require twelve of each in total. Texture each tulip shape on a Cel pad using a veining tool. Keep covered with a thin plastic sheet to prevent drying.

4 Using a flat chisel paint brush start by brushing from the top of the tulip with saphire blue lustre powder. Continue to brush the blue from the outside edges to the centre. Use violet lustre powder to give a second coating of colour, which will highlight the texture.

5 Starting with the largest tulip shape on the bottom tier secure with white royal icing. Secure the second and third tulip ensuring that the middle section is lifted away from the cake. Continue on each of the tiers, and for each remaining side of the cake.

6 Roll out modelling paste as shown in stage one. Lightly dust the square cutters with cornflour then cut out, one hundred and forty five 15mm squares. Forty 12mm squares and fifteen 5mm squares. Allow to harden slightly, then secure to the sides of the cake with soft white royal icing.

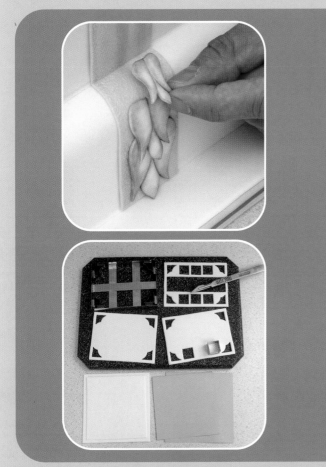

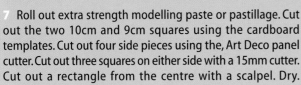

7 Roll out extra strength modelling paste or pastillage. Cut out the two 10cm and 9cm squares using the cardboard templates. Cut out four side pieces using the, Art Deco panel cutter. Cut out three squares on either side with a 15mm cutter. Cut out a rectangle from the centre with a scalpel. Dry.

8 Secure with a little egg white two small flattened spheres onto a piece of 26g white wire cut to the length of the Art Deco panel cutter. Secure on either side a tulip shape as explained in stage three. Secure the side panels with royal icing onto the base. Secure the wired tulips between each panel with a small amount of paste.

Contemporary Hearts

A dramatic and innovative design, featuring a intricate stencilled texture, embossed and highlighted with lustre powder onto the surface of the sugarpaste. The cakes are stacked and tiered to give height and depth to the overall design, with the heart theme being carried through onto the cake top decoration for a striking effect.

Cake sizes
Top tier: round 15cm/6in
(Board size round 20cm/8in drum)

Middle tier: round 20cm/8in
(Board size round 20cm/8in card)

Base: round 25cm/10in
(Board size round 40cm /16in drum)

Completing the cakes
Cover the cakes with almond paste. If you are using a Madeira cake, cover with a thin coating of butter cream prior to covering with the stencil design. Cover the bottom tier board separately with the stencilled sugarpaste design. Position the cakes onto each board. Insert skewers into the bottom tier to support the second tier. Check level of the cake with a spirit level. A stencilled pastillage disc of paste (15cm/6in) has been made to support the perspex separator with the wired glass beads.

♡ Tip
After screeding over the lace stencil mat with the royal icing, lift the stencil with pointed end of the heart facing away from you.

Lightly dust the work surface with icing sugar. Roll out sugarpaste approximately 6mm thick. Ensure that the paste is moveable on the work surface. Lightly grease the smooth side of the floating leaf stencil. Place onto the sugarpaste and roll over with a firm pressure. Brush with super pearl lustre powder.

Brush the cake with alcohol. Lift the paste onto the surface of the cake supported by the rolling pin. Roll across the surface of the cake to remove air bubbles. Peel the stencil away from the sugarpaste. Push the paste against the side of the cake with a plastic side scraper, trimming the surplus paste carefully.

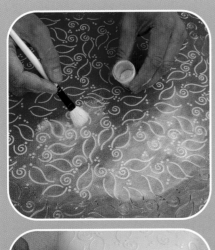

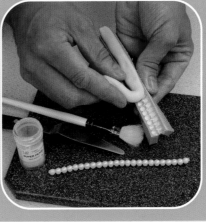

3 Roll out a strip of green modelling paste. Brush with super pearl lustre powder. Roll over with the filigree texture. Cut the width to measure 3cm. Roll up and apply to the base of each cake. Texture white paste with the same texture, brush with super pearl. Cut out forty heart shapes. Secure randomly on the textured sugarpaste.

4 Dust the inside of a 6mm bead mould with super pearl lustre powder. Insert a cylinder of modelling paste and push the mould together. Trim any surplus paste with a small cranked palette knife. Open the mould, and remove the beads. Secure with royal icing directly around the base of each cake.

5 Lightly grease, run out film. Place the smooth side of the heart stencil onto the film. Screed over with royal icing, which has a pinch of gum tragacanth added. Lift the stencil mat carefully. Sprinkle over fairy dust, repeat four times. Dry. Secure along the edge of the filigree textured band with white royal icing using a no.1 piping tube.

6 Roll out green coloured pastillage and then line the inside of two 10cm plastic spheres. Allow both to dry for twelve hours. Join together with green royal icing. Cut out one 8cm disc. Line a 5cm pastry cutter with a 3cm band of pastillage, move the paste within the sphere and pastry cutter during drying to prevent sticking.

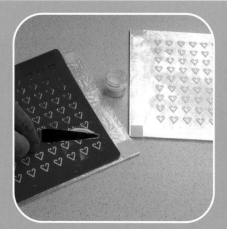

7 Brush embroider the heart shaped design with white royal icing. Make fifteen roses from modelling paste. Make a small cylinder, flatten both edges, fold in half then roll up. Brush with light green lustre powder. Cut out filigree textured heart shapes with the Art Deco leaf cutter, using both cutting sides.

8 Cut out nine hearts. Insert a piece of silver wire and dry. Shape three hearts from silver wire. Tape together. Brush the embroidered hearts with green lustre. Secure sphere onto support with a ball of soft paste underneath to insert the wired hearts. Secure the roses and leaves with white royal icing. Pipe dots between hearts around the base.

Royal Parade

A spherical top tier allows for a great deal of movement to be created with the overall design. The pastillage teardrop pieces reflect the spherical influence both in the flowers used and the general design features. Soft gold and green colours have been used to complement the stylish and airy feel.

Cake sizes
Sphere cake: 15cm/6in
(Cake boards round 18cm/7in drum)

Round: 30cm/12in
(Cake boards round 40cm/16in drum)

Completing the cakes

Cover the sphere in one piece with almond paste. Roll out a light cream coloured sugarpaste and cover in one piece, polishing the surface with a soft ball of the sugarpaste. Cut out a curved section from the round cake and cover as for the sphere. Cover the base cake board with cream coloured sugarpaste. Position the covered cake towards the front edge of the board. Use the cake display stand as a template on the base board. Cut around the base and remove the sugarpaste. The cake stand can then be inserted and the sphere cake displayed. Two sprays of sugar flowers are required to complete decoration.

🍃 Tip
When making the spherical cake use a 23cm/9in cake recipe.

1 Roll out modelling paste to a thickness of 1.5mm. Lightly dust the work surface with cornflour then roll over the entire length with the lattice texture roller. Use a soft brush to apply gold pearl lustre powder. Roll the paste up then secure to the side of the cake.

2 Shape the rose bud from modelling paste. Roll the centre on the edge of your hand tapering to a point. Roll two pieces for either side of the rose. Position the two outer pieces around the centre. Brush the centre with gold pearl and the outside with avocado lustre powder. Repeat, producing twelve in total.

3 Roll out pastillage or extra strength modelling paste thinly. Cut out with the teardrop cutter. Cut the inner sections. Lightly dust a spherical mould with cornflour and open out the teardrop section when inside the sphere. Cut three pieces for each tier. Allow to dry and carefully remove. Clean any rough edges with a small piece of emery paper.

4 Roll out pale green modelling paste thinly. Using the double scroll leaf cutter with the edge lightly dusted with cornflour to cut out six pieces. Reverse the cutter to cut out six further pieces on the opposite cutting edge. Keep the cut out pieces under a plastic covering.

5 Place the cut out pieces onto a piece of absorbent kitchen paper. Brush over the scroll sections with gold green lustre powder. Brush the remaining area with avocado lustre. Continue to keep the cut out pieces covered to prevent drying.

6 The sections are applied to the side of the cake with cream coloured soft royal icing. Start at the front of the cake alternating the pieces as they flow around the side. Try to ensure that each piece appears to flow from one onto the next. Secure the rose shapes with soft royal icing.

7 Repeat stage four for the sphere cake. Cutting out six pieces on each cutting edge. Colour dust as in stage five then secure from the top of the sphere with even spaces between, down the side of the cake. Secure rose shapes between scroll sections.

8 Insert a flower pick into the top of the ball cake and to the right on the bottom tier. Insert the flower sprays. Use firm consistency cream coloured royal icing to secure the three, pastillage teardrop pieces between the flowers. Support with foam sponge until dry. Trim the edge of the boards with ribbon.

Snowflake Flurry

A Snowflake theme has been incorporated into the texture design, and complemented with the cut out sections, highlighted by the use of the fairy dust. The design could also be adapted for a single tier Christmas or festive celebration cake.

Cake sizes
Top tier: round 15cm/6in
(Cake boards round 15cm/6in card)

Base: round 25cm/10in
(Cake boards round 34cm/14in drum)

Completing the cakes
Cover both cakes with almond paste and white sugarpaste allowing it to dry between coats. If using Madeira cake, cover with a thin coating of butter cream prior to coating with the sugarpaste. Place the base cake onto the board and cover the edge with a strip of sugarpaste. Stake the cake to support the top tier with plastic dowels. Secure top tier off set, on the bottom tier. Sugar flowers have been used for the cake top, and are inserted into a small plastic dish of Styrofoam, which has been covered with white modelling paste, and then filigree piped over with a no.1 piping tube and white royal icing.

1 Roll out white modelling paste to 1.5mm in thickness and long enough to go around the side of the cake. Roll over with the snowflake texture. Use a thin cranked palette knife to slide underneath and loosen the paste from the work surface.

2 Lightly dust the work surface with cornflour and place the textured paste onto this. Brush the spaces between the snowflake design with lime sparkle. Brush over each of the snowflakes with light green lustre powder. Brush off excess powder with a large soft brush.

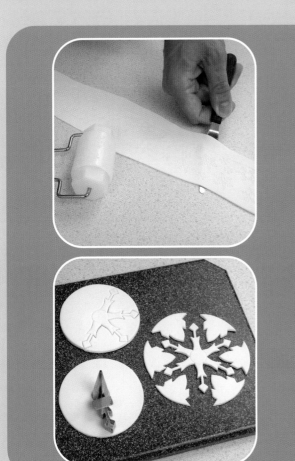

3 Roll out pastillage thinly. Cut out a circle with a 7cm plain pastry cutter. Place the diamanté cutter with the pointed end on the edge of the circle. Mark the centre of the circle with the open end of a piping tube. Lightly dust the cutter with cornflour. Cut out each section on opposite sides. Cut eight or nine snowflakes in total. Dry.

4 Brush the surface of the snowflake with egg white or sugar glue and place onto a piece of paper. Sprinkle fairy dust over. Lift with a palette knife and remove excess. Secure randomly to both tiers with white royal icing.

Snowflake Flurry

Acknowledgements

My wife Karina, for your advice, support and understanding
Clarice Tadd for making some of the cake bases on pages 8 and 32
Lesley Bastone for making the flowers on pages 5, 8 and 11
Christine Brunsch for the Orchids on page 2
Claire Benison Graphic design
Geraldine Randlesome, Creative Cutters, Canada for the inspiration of the stencil mats

Thank you all.
Your help has been greatly appreciated in making this book come to fruition.

British Bakels for supplying the sugarpaste covering used on the cakes
British Bakels Ltd
Granvill Way Bicester Oxon OX26 4JT

Cake stand, pages 5 and17
Available from:
Devon Ladye Products, The studio, Coldharbour, Uffculme, Devon EX15 3EE
Tel: 01884 841316

Cake stand, page 11
Available from:
Cynthia Venn, 3, Anker Lane, Stubbington, Fareham, Hants. P014 3HF
Cynthia.venn@virgin.net

Cake separator, pages 8 and 32
Lindy's Cakes Ltd. Tel: 01296 623906 www.lindyscakes.co.uk

Lustre and sparkle colours used are from VB Sugar Art. Tel: Fax 01505 683689
Silver wires available from: The Old Bakery, Kingston St. Mary, Taunton, Somerset TA2 8HW
Tel : Fax 01823 451205